Bridges Around the World

Understanding Fractions

Elise Wallace

Consultants

Lisa Ellick, M.A.
Math Specialist
Norfolk Public Schools

Pamela Estrada, M.S.Ed.
Teacher
Westminster School District

Publishing Credits

Rachelle Cracchiolo, M.S.Ed., *Publisher*
Conni Medina, M.A.Ed., *Managing Editor*
Dona Herweck Rice, *Series Developer*
Emily R. Smith, M.A.Ed., *Series Developer*
Diana Kenney, M.A.Ed., NBCT, *Content Director*
Stacy Monsman, M.A., *Editor*
Kristy Stark, M.A.Ed., *Editor*
Kevin Panter, *Graphic Designer*

Image Credits: back cover: Peter Phipp/Travelshots.com/Alamy Stock Photo; p.7 (top) CHRISTOPHE SIMON/AFP/Getty Images; p. 8 (bottom right) Archiv Gerstenberg/ullstein bild via Getty Images; p.12 (bottom left) Peter Phipp/Travelshots.com/Alamy Stock Photo; p.15 (bottom) Summerfield Press/CORBIS/Corbis via Getty Images; p.23 (top) Noboru Hashimoto/Corbis via Getty Images; p.25 (bottom left) courtesy of NSW State archives; p.25 (bottom right) Fairfax Media/Getty Images; p.26 Ballymore/REX Shutterstock; p.27 Danjiang Bridge by Zaha Hadid Architects, render by VisualArch

Library of Congress Cataloging-in-Publication Data

Names: Wallace, Elise, author.
Title: Bridges around the world / Elise Wallace.
Description: Huntington Beach, CA : Teacher Created Materials, Inc., [2017] | Series: Engineering marvels | Audience: Grades 4 to 6. | Includes index.
Identifiers: LCCN 2017033191 (print) | LCCN 2017035758 (ebook) | ISBN 9781425859589 (eBook) | ISBN 9781425858124 (pbk.)
Subjects: LCSH: Bridges--Juvenile literature.
Classification: LCC TG148 (ebook) | LCC TG148 .W35 2017 (print) | DDC 624.2--dc23
LC record available at https://lccn.loc.gov/2017033191

Teacher Created Materials

5301 Oceanus Drive
Huntington Beach, CA 92649-1030
http://www.tcmpub.com

ISBN 978-1-4258-5812-4

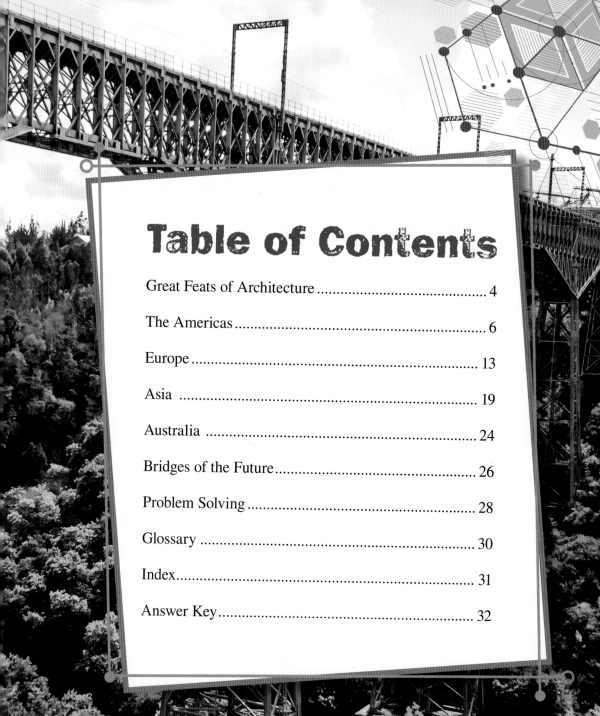

Table of Contents

Great Feats of Architecture

Bridges help people cross great heights. They help people cross water that would otherwise be **inaccessible**. People use them to walk, bike, and drive to new places. Because of bridges, many of the world's wonders become available.

Some bridges are more than a link between two places. They are **feats** of architecture. When we see pictures, we are dazzled by their size. But, when we learn about each **engineering** feat, these bridges become even more awe-inspiring.

The stories of these bridges celebrate **engineers** and **architects**. They show the work of some of the best minds in the world. These people think outside-the-box to create original structures. In doing so, they have helped construct some of the most famous and revered bridges in the world.

But, architects and engineers do not work alone. Many skilled workers help bring their visions to life. From an idea, to a sketch, to a **blueprint**, to a construction site, each great bridge is the work of many minds and countless hours.

The Arthur Ravenel Jr. Bridge is perched above the Cooper River connecting South Carolina cities, Charleston and Mount Pleasant.

The Golden Gate Bridge connects the city of San Francisco to Marin County.

Akashi Kaikyo Bridge crosses over the Akashi Strait in Japan.

The Americas

There are many shining bridges in the Americas. Many of them have changed the future of architecture.

Confederation Bridge

The Confederation Bridge in Canada links Prince Edward Island to New Brunswick. In the past, people could only get to the island by ferryboats. In winter, ice was likely to stop the boats. Some people wanted a bridge. Other people wanted to keep the existing boat system. They did not want people from the **mainland** to have a year-round link to the island. The people voted to settle the issue. Fifty-nine percent of the people voted "yes" to the bridge.

In 1997, the 8-mile (13-kilometer) bridge was finished. It is the longest bridge in the world to span icy waters. Engineers designed the bridge with drivers' safety in mind. They made sure the bridge has curves. Drivers are more likely to stay focused if they need to drive on a curved road rather than a straight one. Engineers also made sure to include thousands of drain ports. These keep water and ice from sitting on the road. With Canada's rainy and snowy seasons, this is a required feature!

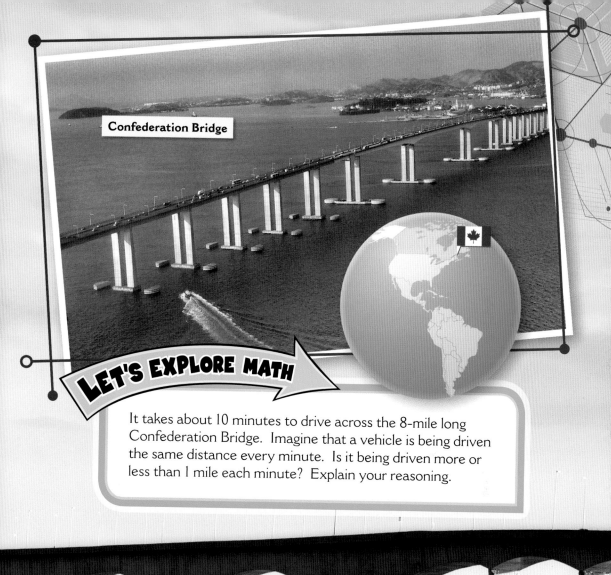

Confederation Bridge

LET'S EXPLORE MATH

It takes about 10 minutes to drive across the 8-mile long Confederation Bridge. Imagine that a vehicle is being driven the same distance every minute. Is it being driven more or less than 1 mile each minute? Explain your reasoning.

Brooklyn Bridge

The Brooklyn Bridge is **iconic**. It spans the East River between Brooklyn and Manhattan in New York City. It was designed by John Augustus Roebling. This **suspension bridge** was the first to use steel cables.

Sadly, Roebling died before building began. His son took over the project. When it was completed in 1883, it was the longest bridge in the world. It has a total length of 5,989 feet (1,825 meters). Each day, thousands of people still cross the Brooklyn Bridge.

Brooklyn Bridge

John Augustus Roebling

Golden Gate Bridge

The Golden Gate Bridge is a suspension bridge in San Francisco, California. Joseph B. Strauss oversaw its construction. He was an engineer. He hired Irving Morrow to help design the bridge. It was finished in 1937.

The main span of the bridge is 4,200 ft. (1,280 m) long. This span is suspended from two cables that join two tall towers. The towers are 746 ft. (227 m) tall.

The bridge has a distinct red-orange hue. No one thought red paint could withstand the salty air. But, Morrow liked the color and found a **durable** paint. The bright color makes the bridge visible even on the foggiest days.

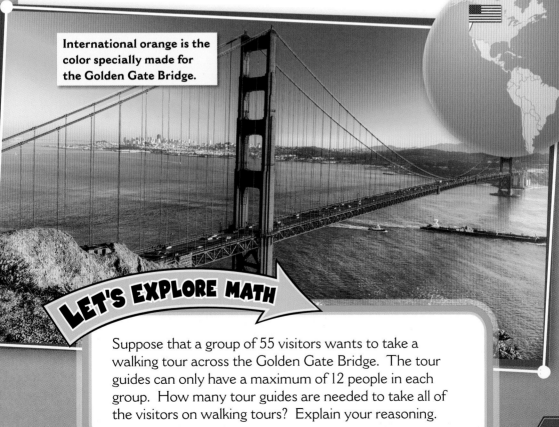

International orange is the color specially made for the Golden Gate Bridge.

LET'S EXPLORE MATH

Suppose that a group of 55 visitors wants to take a walking tour across the Golden Gate Bridge. The tour guides can only have a maximum of 12 people in each group. How many tour guides are needed to take all of the visitors on walking tours? Explain your reasoning.

Malleco Viaduct

Sometimes bridges must cross land instead of water. The Malleco Viaduct is one of Chile's great structures. It has an intriguing history. Built in the late 1800s, the bridge was part of the country's plan to extend its railways.

There was just one problem with the plan: the depth of the Malleco River Valley. The river is 361 ft. (110 m) below the land! To build a railroad, engineers would need to find a way around or over the valley. The choice was clear but not simple. A **viaduct**, or railroad bridge, would have to be constructed. This bridge would cross the valley.

To create this structure, the bridge would need **substantial** support. There are four piers, or pillars, at the center of the bridge. Each pier helps support the weight of the bridge. At each end of the bridge, two stirrups also help bear the weight of the structure. All of the supporting structures are made of steel.

The bridge was completed in 1890. At that time, it was the highest railroad bridge in the world at 333 ft. (101 m). It spans 1,419 ft. (432.5 m) across the valley below.

LET'S EXPLORE MATH

The Malleco Viaduct has 5 equal sections. Imagine that 3 crews are performing maintenance. Use the model to show how they could equally share the work. How much of a section does each crew maintain?

Malleco Viaduct

pier

Tower Bridge

The drawbridge opens for a ship.

Tourists observe the bridge from the glass walkway.

Europe

Lots of structures and buildings in Europe are several centuries old. This is true about Europe's bridges, too. They were built many years ago by ambitious engineers. Each is beautiful and is a tribute to the great minds of the past.

Tower Bridge

The River Thames (TEMZ) is one of the longest rivers in England. Tower Bridge spans the Thames. It has been a distinct feature in London for more than 120 years. It was finished in 1894. Tower Bridge features a double-leaf bascule, or drawbridge. It opens 250 ft. (76 m) to let large ships pass through. Long ago, the bridge was powered by steam. In the last few decades, the drawbridge has been powered by motors.

Today, people can learn more about the bridge by visiting its museum. There, people can stand on a glass walkway above the drawbridge. They see the drawbridge open and close beneath them. The bridge's old steam engines can be viewed in the museum, too. Visitors can get close to view items from the bridge's history!

Pont du Gard

Pont du Gard is a bridge that is a work of art. And, it is over 3,000 years old! The bridge resides in southern France. But, it was constructed by the Romans. Long ago, France was part of the Roman Empire. The Romans were great engineers and built many structures.

Roman buildings often include **arches**. Arches provide strong structural support. The Pont du Gard has three tiers of arches that cross the River Gard. It was constructed as an **aqueduct** to transport fresh water.

Ponte Vecchio

Ponte Vecchio is in Florence, Italy. The name means "old bridge." It was engineered by Taddeo Gaddi and was built in 1345. Gaddi was also a famous artist. Today, the bridge is a well-known landmark.

Arches support this bridge, too. But, these arches are not like the Roman arches. The Roman arches are full semi-circles. The arches on the Ponte Vecchio are not full semicircles. They are called segmental arches. This type of arch was invented in the later part of the Middle Ages, after the fall of the Roman Empire. The arches give the bridge's waterway a spacious feel. This allows boats to easily travel under the bridge.

LET'S EXPLORE MATH

Today, the Pont du Gard is a popular place for tourists to visit. A restaurant at the site even features fresh waffles.

1. Imagine that 6 tourists want to share 4 waffles. Draw a picture showing how they can equally share the waffles.

2. How much of a waffle does each tourist get?

3. How is your answer related to the division problem 4 ÷ 6?

Pont du Gard

Ponte Vecchio's segmental arches

Taddeo Gaddi

15

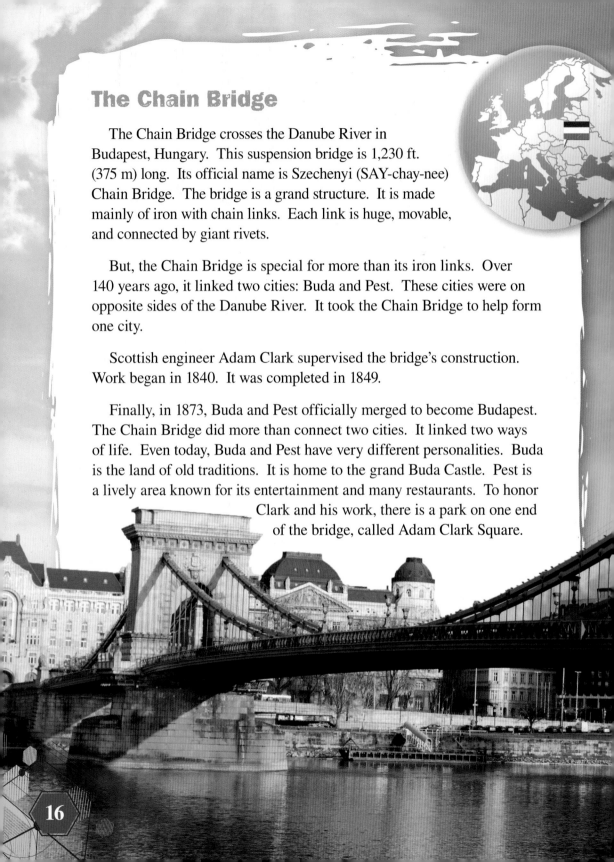

The Chain Bridge

The Chain Bridge crosses the Danube River in Budapest, Hungary. This suspension bridge is 1,230 ft. (375 m) long. Its official name is Szechenyi (SAY-chay-nee) Chain Bridge. The bridge is a grand structure. It is made mainly of iron with chain links. Each link is huge, movable, and connected by giant rivets.

But, the Chain Bridge is special for more than its iron links. Over 140 years ago, it linked two cities: Buda and Pest. These cities were on opposite sides of the Danube River. It took the Chain Bridge to help form one city.

Scottish engineer Adam Clark supervised the bridge's construction. Work began in 1840. It was completed in 1849.

Finally, in 1873, Buda and Pest officially merged to become Budapest. The Chain Bridge did more than connect two cities. It linked two ways of life. Even today, Buda and Pest have very different personalities. Buda is the land of old traditions. It is home to the grand Buda Castle. Pest is a lively area known for its entertainment and many restaurants. To honor Clark and his work, there is a park on one end of the bridge, called Adam Clark Square.

LET'S EXPLORE MATH

The Chain Bridge is about 15 meters wide. It is divided into 2 lanes. How wide is each lane? Represent your answer using meters.

the Chain Bridge

Helix Bridge's open design lets people see the city lights.

Asia

Asia is also home to many amazing bridges. Some of them are new creations that look futuristic. Others are ancient designs with long histories.

Helix Bridge

Singapore's Helix Bridge is unlike any bridge in the world. It has a double helix design that resembles the structure of **DNA**. It gives the bridge a unique look. The design also helped builders use less steel than they normally use.

The bridge is about 919 ft. (280 m) long. The bottom of the bridge is 29 ft. (9 m) above the water. This height allows boats to easily pass.

The bridge opened on April 24, 2010. Many bridges are made for cars, trucks, and buses. But, Helix Bridge is only for **pedestrians**. The bridge has five large platforms for visitors to stop to look at the views. People can see the city's skyline and Marina Bay from these platforms. At night, the bridge is an impressive sight. It sparkles with colorful LED lights.

Chengyang Bridge

Chinese builders have constructed bridges for thousands of years. However, Chengyang Bridge was built about a hundred years ago in 1916. Yes, that may sound like a long time ago. But, it is not that long when you consider that many Chinese structures date back 6,000 years!

The bridge is a wind and rain bridge because it has a canopy that protects visitors from wind, rain, and other weather. Many bridges in China are built this same way.

Like Helix Bridge, Chengyang Bridge is only meant for people, not vehicles. It is about 210 ft. (64 m) in length. And, it is 33 ft. (10 m) in height. It is only about 11 ft. (3 m) wide. Even so, the bridge is impressive for reasons other than its size.

Chengyang Bridge

...dge has five pagodas,
...owers. There are
...nd benches for people
...nd enjoy the views.
...ture is mainly made
...ut no rivets or nails
... to secure the pieces.
...ieces are interlocked
...ail joints. These joints
...bridge sturdy.

pagoda

...ail joints

EXPLORE MATH

...agine that 4 visitors want to equally share 11 feet of walking
...ace as they cross Chengyang Bridge.

1. How many feet of walking space will each visitor get?
2. Draw a picture to prove your solution.
3. Write a division equation to represent the situation.

Pearl Bridge

A huge earthquake shook Japan on January 17, 1995. It destroyed Kobe (KO-bay), one of Japan's busiest cities. Each second of the earthquake caused more and more chaos. Cars were thrown. Buildings toppled. Highways collapsed.

Pearl Bridge, also known as Akashi (UH-ka-she) Strait Bridge, was affected, too. It was under construction at the time of the earthquake. The earthquake caused terrible damage to the city. And, it forced engineers to rethink the bridge's design. The bridge had two towers that supported the structure. The earthquake pushed apart those towers. The engineers knew that they would need to make the bridge stronger.

Pearl Bridge took 10 years to rebuild. At the time of its completion in 1998, it became the longest suspension bridge in the world. It is 12,831 ft. (3,911 m) long. Its two towers are 928 ft. (283 m) tall.

The bridge can endure winds up to 180 miles (290 kilometers) an hour and severe pressure from storms and **seismic** activity. In strong winds or storms, the bridge may expand or contract several feet in a day.

Pearl Bridge lays in ruin after the 1995 earthquake.

Australia

Locals call it the "coat hanger" bridge. It is officially called the Sydney Harbour Bridge. It is one of the world's longest steel arch bridges. It spans 1,650 ft. (503 m).

The bridge was built by the Sydney Opera House. Today, both are iconic pieces of the city's skyline. But back in 1912, the idea to build a suspension bridge across Sydney Harbour was just that—an idea. John Bradfield, an engineer, submitted a **cantilever**, or long beam, design for the bridge. It was accepted. But, the project was put on hold when World War I started.

Sydney Opera House

Sydney Harbour Bridge

Once the war ended, steel was available to make the bridge. The architects wanted the bridge to support a lot of weight. They chose a sturdy design that featured steel arches. They used this design instead of Bradfield's. However, he was chosen to oversee the bridge's construction. It was finished in 1932.

The bridge was built without **scaffolding**, or temporary supports. These supports could not be used because the harbor was too deep! Instead, each side of the bridge was built at the same time. Workers constructed the bridge on each side of the bay. They met in the middle and connected the two sides.

John Bradfield

Sydney Harbour Bridge under construction

Bridges of the Future

All over the world, engineers plan for the future. They design new bridges and buildings. Many designs are unlike any that have been seen before.

In London, England, architects have proposed a water bridge. This "sky pool" will connect two apartment buildings. People will be able to swim across the bridge. It is expected to be finished in 2018.

Plans have been made for a unique bridge in Taiwan. It will be called the Danjiang (DAN-gee-ang) Bridge. Its engineers hope to break records. The bridge will be 3,000 ft. (914 m) long and will be supported by only a single tower.

This artist's design shows a "sky pool" connecting two buildings.

Danjiang Bridge

There are many other bridges being designed. Like those that came before, they will connect communities. Each bridge will be designed to inspire people, too.

Of course, each design may present challenges and problems. But, today's engineers will work to solve those problems. They will address any challenges they face, so they can complete each new bridge. In doing so, they will add new wonders to skylines. They will give people new places to visit, too.

Problem Solving

Congratulations! Your engineering firm has been hired to design a highway bridge over a large valley. City council wants to understand the details about the bridge being planned for the community. So, it submits a list of questions for you to answer. Use the bridge specifications to answer them.

Bridge Specifications

- Length: 1,200 meters
- Height: 60 meters
- Width: 36 meters
- Number of Lanes: 8

1. How wide is each lane?

2. You are planning to include five toll booths. How many lanes will each toll booth serve?

3. You are planning to install a concrete pillar every 90 meters to support the length of the bridge. How many bridge supports will there be?

4. The metal beams inside each vertical bridge support are 28 meters long. How many beams will be inside each support?

5. This bridge is going to be busy. The transportation department estimates that there will be about 6,200 vehicles on the bridge each hour. About how many vehicles is this per minute?

Glossary

aqueduct—a structure used to carry water

arches—parts of curves

architects—people who design buildings

blueprint—a plan that shows how something will be built

cantilever—a piece of wood or metal that sticks out from a structure to support the weight above

DNA—deoxyribonucleic acid; material in a cell's nucleus

dovetail—a joint used to connect two pieces of wood

durable—the ability to stay strong and in good condition for a long time

engineering—designing and creating products, systems, or structures by using tools, materials, mathematics, and science

engineers—people who use mathematics and science to solve problems

feats—acts to show great skill and courage

iconic—well-known

inaccessible—difficult or impossible to be reached

mainland—a large area of land that does not include islands

pedestrians—people who travel on foot

scaffolding—metal poles and wooden boards used to build or support

seismic—caused by an earthquake

substantial—large amount

suspension bridge—a bridge hung from two or more cables that are held up by towers

viaduct—a long, high bridge that carries a road or railroad over something

Index

Answer Key

Let's Explore Math

page 7:

Less than 1 mile per minute; Explanations will vary, but may include that if the vehicle is driven 1 mile for each of 10 minutes, 10 miles will be traveled. Only 8 miles are traveled. So, the vehicle must be moving less than 1 mile each minute.

page 9:

5 tour guides; Explanations will vary, but may include that 12 visitors × 4 tour guides is 48 visitors, so another tour guide is needed for the 7 remaining visitors.

page 10:

$\frac{5}{3}$, or $1\frac{2}{3}$ sections; Models will vary. Example:

1	2	3	1	2	3	1	2	3

page 14:

1. Models will vary. Example:

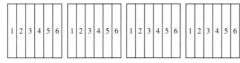

2. $\frac{4}{6}$ of a waffle

3. It is related because 4 waffles are being divided among 6 tourists and $4 \div 6$ is $\frac{4}{6}$.

page 17:

$7\frac{1}{2}$ m

page 21:

1. $2\frac{3}{4}$ ft., or $\frac{11}{4}$ ft.

2. Pictures will vary. Example:

1	2	3	4	1	2	3	4	1234	1234	1234

3. $11 \div 4 = \frac{11}{4}$ or $2\frac{3}{4}$

Problem Solving

1. $\frac{36}{8} = 4\frac{4}{8}$ m, or $4\frac{1}{2}$ m

2. $\frac{8}{5} = 1\frac{3}{5}$ lanes

3. $\frac{1,200}{90} = 13\frac{30}{90}$, or $13\frac{1}{3}$; 14 bridge supports

4. $\frac{60}{28} = 2\frac{4}{28}$, or $2\frac{1}{7}$ beams

5. $\frac{6,200}{60} = 103\frac{20}{60}$, or $103\frac{1}{3}$; 103 or 104 vehicles per minute